Also by Alice Derry:

Poetry
Stages of Twilight
Getting Used to the Body (chapbook)
Clearwater
Not As You Once Imagined (chapbook)
Strangers to Their Courage
Translations of Rilke's New Poems (chapbook)
Tremolo
Hunger

Essays
Around the Salish Sea, Plants and Art, Folio I, with Fred
Sharpe and Laurel Moulton

website: www.alicederry.com

Asking

poems

ALICE DERRY

MoonPath Press

Poetry
ISBN 978-1-936657-69-8

Cover art: *Stalking Poppies* by Josie Gray

Author photo by Charlotte Watts

Book design by Tonya Namura, using Kristi (display) and
Baskerville (text).

MoonPath Press, an imprint of Concrete Wolf Poetry Series,
is dedicated to publishing the finest poets
living in the U.S. Pacific Northwest.

MoonPath Press
PO Box 445
Tillamook, OR 97141

MoonPathPress@gmail.com

http://MoonPathPress.com

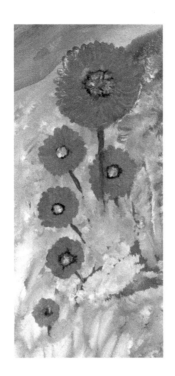

Bruce

Acknowledgments

Cloudbank: "Division"

Catamaran: "Reprieve"

Hubbub: "In Rain" (Under the title "Rural" this poem won the Vi Gale Award of $500)

Windfall: "Clearwater Again"

Sextant: "When You are Lost the World" and "On the Elwha"

Accepted by Saginaw Valley State University: "At the Edge of a Dream"

Cirque: "Snowshoeing" and "*The Genesis of Life Lay Deep and Anticipant Under the Sky, 1944*" (The latter poem nominated by *Cirque* for the Pushcart Prize)

The Madrona Project: "Lost and Found"

Poetry East: "Those Were the Times"

Cascadian Zen: "Celestial" and "A Quarter Note"

My deepest gratitude to friends who made this book possible: Charlotte Warren, for help over years, each poem and its many revisions, and readings of the manuscript; Tess Gallagher, for detailed comments twice on the entire manuscript, and suggesting the book's title; Joe Powell, for detailed comments on earlier drafts of the manuscript; Kate Reavey, for comments on individual poems and a reading of the manuscript; Gary Copeland Lilley, for a reading of the manuscript. Many thanks to Lana Hechtman Ayers for her continued belief in my poems.

For support through the loss of my husband and continued belief in my writing: these friends and also Barbara Drake and Bill Beckman, Bill Siverly,

Molly Gloss, Lucia Perillo, Jane Mead, Kim and Perrin Stafford, Kathryn and Geo Hunt, Stan Rubin, Pamela Murphy, Eycke Strickland, Suzie Bennett, and Sissi Bruch. My love and thanks to my five brothers and families. My especial love and gratitude to my daughter, Lisel, for her constant support, and to Ron and Ronan Murdock-Perriera.

Table of Contents

Asking

Requiem

for my husband, Bruce, 1942-2014

Across the canyon thousands of maples
let down their green-white flowers,
and a light the color of hope
moves in April's new spring twilight,
layers the deep points, the high points,
all of it hovering—all of it bare
beginning, growth-heat's hesitation
against the cold.

A timid insistence, this burgeoning—
beside it, your quiet subtraction,
your soft, unremarkable departure,
giving in to gravity's pull,
felling you. No one there
to hear the sound.

Requiem: 1

If I knew how to keen, I would.
            Pearl Gleage

Speaking…to the dead is too difficult for a mouth…
            Toni Morrison

On the Elwha

I could not see to see.
Emily Dickinson

Since you've become nothing,
I drift in a kind of homelessness.
Purpose eludes me, the house
domesticity built.

As these corridors of maples
climb toward the river bluffs,
April's confirming sun glances
off sword ferns to obscure them.

Not to see, when you are gone,
the one I want visible,
to squint up corridors
into a wall of light: I don't mind.

I could live in opaque light,
polish of trillium
on these Salish lowlands,
of fawn and chocolate lilies.

What hovers around me today
as each leaf unfolds
is the aura I create
when missing haunts me.

Nothing here offers more
than what is, and illusion—
the river, transformed as fire,
wind moving the tall trunks to moan.

What Will You Do?

people keep asking,
but I'm wrapped in the garments of your non-being,
what continues between us,

shrouded, full of question,
nothing when I look but space.

I felt your night-gone body, your face,
your shoulder, small pats and kisses,
but hesitant, the center
dark inside you.

They didn't give me long before
they closed you in the black bag. Your body
    hardening
which in days would be soft to the earth's
ministrations.

When we first lived together, afraid you might die
and I would lose you, my heart
ached from the fright of loving with such abandon.
We lived past that, past generosity—into the
    quicksand
of finding too much fault,

and all the time, something deepening around us
holding more than we perceived
until you left, necessarily taking
part of me with you.

A minus world, kingdom without touch.
Absence the pillar I lean on.

Division

A raven wings from a tree, like shadow.

The same yearling doe as last week keeps her place
    in the field browsing,
her eyes, her ears on me. Broken from her mother,
a constant trot to keep up, then silence, her companion,
closes around her.
Is she every day alone, fully at one with her grasses?
She doesn't seek further.

I do—to come to terms with what's been taken
when the giving was like these June evenings,
sun tilted our way. You thrived—
willow, wren, rose, disclosed as light.
Gold-breasted swallows swooped for insects
    we set to motion.
Warblers insistent.

Think of the old saying, *you won't be given more
    than you can bear,*
meaning suffering, or maybe it's happiness,
not more than would break you apart.

And because the weeping tenderness of my girlhood
was blunted, I can stand this much pain?

Folk wisdom would rather give any reason for anguish,
    even judgment,
than live side by side with the great marsh hawk,
rising in angled cuts on the currents
to dip down like rainbow's end, somewhere
neither of us can know.

Vetch purples the meadows.

Whatever it divided is taking down the old fence,
first loosening posts year by rain year,
then picking at the wood heaps,
mud and moss, beetle and worm erasing them
into earth. Salal takes over the watered post hollows,
adding its six inches of new green each year.

Flourishing.
Soon I will walk a new path.

No words now.
You only had to put your hand on my shoulder,
turn me to you, releasing permission
that what I could offer was worthwhile.

Early Obsidian

Right before dusk,
moon's risen,
its half-self too bright
because of winter's
early obsidian.

What passes for sunset,
washed out, still gilds
the laden trees.
I crunch through
fast-freezing crust,
myself glossed.

I hope it was that way
for you—candy bar
laid out on your carseat,
once you'd put your time in
with chainsaw and firelogs—

That you savored
spring light slinging its arm
around you.
And before you fell,
you looked up—beyond
sun, beyond blue.

Requiem: II

O, this is the poison of deep grief.
      Hamlet, 4.5.75

      the way candlelight licks
the night clean until one of us is gone.
            Tess Gallagher

Your Death Invades Me

After childhood's sweet nuzzling—
laps and circling arms—desire
takes over, so coveted,
it can tip to guilt and shame.

We don't allow ourselves to want,
or longing too painful,
we deny.

In the novel, though, I got the feeling
the older man's need for warmth
could surpass sex,
if that were required to have her,
the feral woman.

Well, he wasn't beyond,
neither of them was,
but the book holds out that possibility.

Your death invades me
with a kind of earth-sickness
Erdrich describes—so in love
with your transformation,

I might be like the old man,
just happy to know you, untouchable
as you travel outside desire.

Infused with death's fever, I could reach
to where you've quit becoming—
my losing the comfort of day into night into day

to the possibility I might still be part of you.
As in the novel, nothing like that
happens.

They made their child, those fluent afternoons.

I lie on the couch. Summer heat
invades me. It's your arms-around-me
I want.

At the Edge of a Dream,

something said *Bruce Murdock*,
and you stood there, shy,
a little reluctant, your face,
its appeal of ironic humor.

That's all. Only a few seconds
of half-sleep when you
might come to me.

For those first months,
I never wanted to think
about poetry again.

Solace was the green mist of wonder
our maples spread
over the valley, rain days,
fog days, exhaling
their flowers' firm, white-green belief
in the next season.

Words poured out anyway.
For all the flowers' translucence,
after dark, it was *words,*
words, words.

You loved how they
hoard their uneasy jokes over centuries—
deep inside *partner,*
the French for *partition,*

double-faced *cleave,* most tender,
most brutal.

When *wind* softens, *winds*
its shadow through sun's revelations,
winding sheet on my tongue.

If words were our yawing anchor,
I drift now.
Their rescue lay between us.

Oh, the cold days a spring can stoop to,
right after a week of deceptive warmth.
The maples have plenty of time
for shaking out their folded leaves.

Snowshoeing

Sometimes the overcast light
mutes firs and hemlocks
bluing toward the high peaks,
as if there were no speech.

Even when sky gradually
mackerels, tacit light bars the sun
behind a thin dullness,
the other side of grief.

Without reluctance, I let
the hours pass farther and farther
from you, stare across
the muffled scene.

Acceptance.
Mist, rising from the river valleys,
freezes. Behind my eyes,
the burning doesn't overflow.

Ghosts

Queen. Whereon do you look?
Hamlet. On him, on him!...Do you see nothing there?
Queen. Nothing at all, yet all that is I see.
    Hamlet, 3.4.124-133

1
Day's light is expectation.
My body, too long still,
asks to move.

The visible, changed;
invisible, just that.

Grief for you wakes what I carry—
now a stone, now a beating heart,
I'm here, I'm here.
But nothing is.

2
You couldn't *not* be, the self
I woke to each morning,
sweet flesh I tasted,
body and mind one *importunity*.

We built a life of those words
until we reached the place
couples hardly need to speak.

Where words had been,
aery nothing,
still gave us *habitation*.

3
And if Hamlet's
grief within, which passes show
has brought his father's ghost,

well, appearance
is mutable.

4
Reason-riven, Hamlet
kills, is killed.

In my dream, I race over the hills,
wolves behind me, snapping.

In my dream, you are putting down
the dining room floor I wanted.

At first all goes well, then the boards
swell out of shape,

then turn to waves,
then rot and dissolve.

5
Fall morning light, visibly
waning.
Invisible, his longing,
my longing:
On him! On him!

ghosts

Then he cannot speak because there is that patch of shadow again, vibrating at the edge of light.
         Maaza Mengiste, The Shadow King

    Remember thee?
Ay, thou poor ghost, whiles memory holds a seat
in this distracted globe.
         Hamlet, 1.5.95-97

I Wake, Then Drift

You died in April, light and growth
arguing your energy had not been lost
but funneled into the greening.

You didn't believe that and neither do I.
No great immensity passed over me,
no dirt clods ceremoniously thudded down.
In a world crowded with living,
you were made a handful of ashes.

Hardly enough to justify Laertes' young fire, shouting,
Now pile your dust upon the quick and dead,
as he leaped into Ophelia's grave, Hamlet after,
not to be outdone in love. How we leaned almost
out of our seats, watching Shakespeare balance tears
on the edge of the ridiculous.

Two dawns in a row, I wake, then drift in a tiny margin,
standing where the door which opened for you, opens.
More than dreaming, I insist, your actual self.
Then gone.

No time to speak to the armored ghost in his leaving.

Of course I want to squeeze through—another glance,
a chance to say something.
Wanting so much, as when I first met you—
I tried to hold back to make sure you were the right
      one—

then leaned into you from our heat-sleep.
Darling, I said.

You no longer have to worry about *wanting*,
how it forces a life
to wake up and get out of bed.

Leaves on the canyon maples still reflect sun
    this November.
By evening, I face the crescent, which waxes,
pushing me along. Slow enough.
Even Hamlet only saw his ghost once more.

Lost and Found

Then practice losing farther, losing faster
  Elizabeth Bishop

I lost sunset. I lost the stars, fog returning.
On darkening sand, I found a mottled eagle feather.
That will be for Theresa, her weaving.

I've lost all the nights to come, camping with you.
Without your shoulders, my narrow one-person tent
is all I can carry. Coffin tent, I call it,
to go with my mummy bag.

I don't know yet what I've found—
where the two big opposites, land and sea, edge
    together
among a scatter of drift logs, shells, and spongy
    seaweed carpets,
ruckus of birds and surf. Nothing changes
but each moment feels different.

I don't know yet if I've found what I can live with.
You aren't scuffing this sand beside me,
our first courtship hike together.
But I have no way to lose you in the echoes of the
    night years later
when we couldn't sleep for sea lions' barking.

I keep looking to agree with someone—
shall we hike now, shall we eat, nap in the tent?
If I step without you into the unknown, I might find
    it possible.

Sanderlings rise as one body, their strict formation aloft.
They are never alone, landing to stilt-run the tide line.
Unconcerned, a ragged stretch of oystercatchers inks
    the gray.

I am *one* here, speak to no one except any hiker's hello.

The second morning, I lost the promised sun, straggling
    out of my tent
into mist. Glad my stove worked.

What found me were four river otters, sleek in the
    waves. On sand,
their tails weighty, they tumbled forward,
then back. Once I froze to driftwood,
they dashed to their creek-side den.

I followed the tideline until rain came.

I missed you every moment—how much you hated
    camping in sand,
how many times you came anyway for the wild of it.

The wild rose up in me, as it does when I go into it,
    expecting nothing
and on the friendly beach make my frail home against
    a bank, under scaled spruce,
among sea-rocket. They aren't letting me or refusing me.

Losing doesn't allow itself to be pure and unatoned.
Finding, no compensation, pours like flood tide onto the
    beach.

We know the living and dead are entwined, but here,
    where I am never
without tide's losing and finding,
why should the twining be so finally unknowable?

Like Rilke's lovers, we lay here that first time, all the
    wildness loose in us, thinking
ourselves one,
thinking no further than one.

Deepening of a May Night

How visible the world becomes
when one we love is taken from it.

Mist wraps house and valley,
rain-saturated earth returning
what it cannot hold.

I see deeper, as spring extends
even on an evening obscured.
Nothingness also a shape.

This afternoon, hail's shrapnel
felled the tulips.

That you died a month ago
doesn't keep coltsfoot
from usurping the roadsides'
ragged verges.

When that door opened,
you were drawn into *the unknown country*.
This world shuddered, realigned itself.

Hidden from me all the years,
that you were the shield, making
private life around our wood-burning stove,
its flowering heat, small dailiness.

Eyes unveiled, I have lost
the ordinary warmth of flannel.
A way to collect myself.

Like you, each new child makes
the dangerous crossing over a threshold.
The difference—we can succor:
warm flesh, feed hunger.

I don't know how to hold you.
Nothing you are, I am.

At Deer Park

that if you would love a woman without ever
looking back on your love as a folly,
she must die while you are courting her.
  George Eliot, *Adam Bede*

The prospect changes as I turn and twist on the ridge,
losing whole groups of mountains.
Phlox, your favorite, adds shades of lavender.
Through the lily galleries, yellow, then white.

Fog pours over the ridgetop, opens for sun,
then freezes around me, like the shivering rhythm of
      grief.

This spine of basalt unwinds at the end of the road.
Where it begins, just above the sea, you were
      building a house.
Come live with me there, you said.

So we drove often into our mountains, even for late
      evening strolls,
long chats broken by the high peaks inviting silence.
We argued down this trail, our utter stubbornness
on two sides of something.

Rain sweeps Maiden Peak now, a smatter, a small
      drench,
and moves east. On days of still heat,
we lazed, full of stories and lies,
had the thing called happiness in its brief
unbelievable minutes.

There is a heightening here—a jolt
dissolving me into the whole.
I can't be still enough, while the hilltopping swallowtails
span their swift rags of sunshine,
males prowling for females.
Or does it just seem that way?

The one goal is togetherness—beyond even food and
     drink—
to be completed with another.

Shining like Winter Twilight

I stood
on the library's street corner
shivering in my required
schoolgirl dress, sockless.
Never sure if my parents

would pick me up
after the library closed,
couldn't count on dinner,
or space
to do homework—

even in the half of my life
with you,
when you made sure
I had coats and mittens,
hot meals, could drive myself

so I didn't have to wait—
I was still afraid of twilight.
As I steered home after work
in layers of pink and purple,
scared

I wouldn't have enough time.
Losing you, I've lost *next*.
I'm stalled in winter sunset
edging the mountains
with gold,

a promise of lingering.
I stand, a girl in crusted snow.
Until, inch by inch,
the descent
of unseeable darkness.

Reprieve

This horned lark climbs
the small hillocks of fescue,
then descends into dirt valleys,
hidden by grass.

I want it to turn toward me,
show its secret V black vest
so I can say, *horned lark all right*,
but it's doing the necessary, seeds and
small beetles, the path they've laid out,
keeping course without a name.

You taught me these ridgewalks:
start high and stay high.
Although all we inhaled was mountain air.

Today, as if I were with you, harebells
purple the hills, signaling the end to bloom.
As if you were still here—
Olympus on one side, Needles the other.
Zero chance of rain.

I had to fight for my ten minutes
with your body.
I was still crying, no, still trying
to overcome who knows what
to get myself to reach out and touch you.
Your hair soft, able to be brushed aside.
To do what the ages have done: lay my wet,
    breathing lips
on your stone skin, muster you once more
in the salvaged jacket you'd worn to a rag.

The sheriff wanted me away from you.
And what good would it be to stay?
Starting high, along the ridgetops, above treeline,
where rock buckled as one plate
shoved against another, you felt you'd gotten back
some of what you deserved.

The air unencumbered. Nothing hedged you in.
Some days a door opens.
Others, it's the simple emptiness of the universe.

Celestial

Quiet inside yourself.
Quiet.
Where I find you, husband,
if not in the tossed-aside work gloves,
if not in the drawer
I haven't cleared of your things.

Yes, inside.
Where you still reign
like this January super moon
hovering close.
Since the clouds have gone
to ice, it's haloed
in rainbow. That's

memory.

Seasons

O who can be
both moth and flame?
Theodore Roethke

She is a girl who has been split and what stands here is both
flesh and shadow, bone and silhouette, no more than air filled
with smoke.

Maaza Mengiste, The Shadow King

In Rain

I curve between flooded fields
until I find the tundra swans,
stopping to snip greens on their way north.

We loved poking along these country roads,
ditches weedy with forget-me-not run wild.

We even loved the tumbled-down places
with one pathetic horse—someone's try
at country living.

Swooping up the hogback, we rolled down
to black cows grazing near pavement.
Himalaya clumps, Steve's apple farm.

Any day, at least half the world has to be grieving.
Parents, lost partners, and please don't let me think
    of it,
children. No wonder we stagger.

You come to me strangely, as water seeping
through earth is stripped clean.
This glimpse as we get ready for a party:
late, gift not wrapped, can't find clothes.
My usual anxiety dream.

And then you're lowering yourself into a hot bath
and soaping all over. *Can I wash my face?* I ask,
kneeling there. *Yes, anything you want,*
and you've brought my own soap dish
so I know you mean it.

Washing my face in dream, as if
I don't know how, I'm right next to your thigh,
warm and reddened from bath water.

Why don't I take off my clothes, slide in beside you?
I'm awake in morning light.
And now I'm leaving the swans

to ramble back roads in pelting rain,
which is going to go on for days, cutting down
the new crocus before they can open, melting
	everything.

What use is all this missing?
Even to admit my whole self is consumed
by what we were, what we're not,
is understatement.

The cold rain's washing spring in.
My dream of beginning so different:
to insist on warmth we're both touching
					at the same time.

Your Purple Shirt

In June evening's full daylight, I crunch gravel
on the road by the bird refuge, imagine families at
    supper
where I'd like to be with you, watching Rachel
    Maddow,
the left-wing hype we digested, once we'd cleared
our plates. She was still talking the night you died.

Domesticity: I fought for it, gave up much of my life
to have a predictable dinner hour, no demands,
just slippers and jeans in our old-fashioned kitchen,
like Aunt Rose's. Over our scarred floors, sink to stove,
I risked that journey. As she did. For her it ended
in violence called "the private life."

Islands of Nootka roses, their great briar impenetrable,
anchor these ocean uplands. I skirt the edges—
confident profusion, spicy scent elusive
as sun-soaked fir in the mountains.
Breathe and it's there, breathe, it's gone.
Let me try one flower at a time, since each
opens, pours forth, and is still.
A bee might go mad, I would think, but they are all
buzzing intention, rose to rose,
sensibly hived now at dusk.

I cling to their mysteries, but like you,
they tell me nothing. I'll always taste
at the edge of your death, grief
pouring forth, then still—

this evening missing too much your purple shirt with
     pearl snaps
I threw away, along with the navy chamois you always
     wore
although you preferred green. When I get home,
I'll take them out of the waiting trash.

I don't know either why at the end you suddenly let weeks
go by without showering until I smelled you in the room
and was afraid. You could always
fend off questions.

Before that, six-thirty on endless June evenings,
you and I talked in the fearless light.
Your answers implicit when I asked:
Where should I go? Who should I be?

I Stand in Color,

bloom-crowded meadows,
paintbrush, larkspur, golden lily, each finding space.
I'm in one field, looking, then I've come to the next.

You've taken with you my fear of wilt—
rhody's wet tissue wadded under its bush.

You stood for simple emptiness, the universe as process
without mercy. What you always told me.
I slowed us down, making you wait
until I stared long enough to lose myself
in each flower's exuberant rush,
reckless squander of beauty.

My only comfort this first lonely summer—
flowers as they are, in their seasonal turning.

Is it because you are dead, plants have lost their
        holiness?
Or have I joined their quiet indifference?
But no, their patience exceeds me, opening and closing
their millions of stomata—*mouths*, people say,
like our mouths, but ours is a different hunger.

Watchful, keeping loss contained,
I can't allow myself the cushion to leave
disbelief, and if I stumble, return to you.

Spring's quicksilver has run to ground—
cold nights which blossom to blue days,
fawn lilies and trillium mocking the dark woods.

Maples have left off their ardent mating,
bundles of helicopter seeds embracing flight

as the trees shed every flower part no longer needed.
Bleeding heart forget their complex valentines, inch
    forth
rust slippers of seeds.

I cling to the heart. Set in motion when a body
is barely seeded, it beats, most often silently,
no symbol. Yet we let it ache and long. What the heart
wants is love. Abandoned, it persists, asking.

A Quarter Note

In the funnel of their leaves
over the winding canal road,
igniting the firs' dark hood,
October dusk dropping,
maybe I do feel bigleaf maples'
final shine before the fall.

Maybe I do see a glimpse
of our old life together.
While you drove, smoothing
the car through its curves,
I could listen
for yellow's quarter note

in the red's deep gong.
Risk that. *Don't be silly,*
you'd say. But I was,
you there, and I, careful
to hear the music, since anytime
might be the last.

At the Bird Refuge

Carrying the secure anchor of grief
    Hilma Wolitzer

I know your mind and heart,
a friend says, but he doesn't.
This small February sun knows it,
dissolving the fog bank.
Onto the globes of rosehips—
some blasted past fall prime—
it pastes the light, this little sun
I want to lie down and roll in.

The more I say,
Yes, it's been a terrible time
What a great guy he was
Thank you for thinking of us,
the more he talks over me
because he wants to have said the special,
truly comforting thing.

Rosethorn and towhee,
sparrow and field grass.
This prescient blue affirms
the end of snow, not enough
to swell our rivers in July.
Grieving too might leave me.
Then it will just be emptiness.

I'm jealous that he bicycles on
with his still-blond wife,
not that young, but athletic.
I was braving my walk, I was taking heart
in the habit of rosehips and lichen,
their heedless loyalty.

My heart has no way to be known,
doesn't want to be coaxed there.
Once roused, it might blast the skies
with its wailing.
Don't try now, friend.
Carry on, willow and saskatoon,
shorn of your leaves.

Harvest

A certain convocation of politic worms
are e'en at him.
        Hamlet, 4.3.20

Jim dead, Dick, Judith, Tony, even Barbara's
two dogs a week apart. Only half over,
November stores up its bounty.

Dying in spring was your last great gift—
all of summer's long-candled nights
to get ready.

I've gathered a ripening, many days
lying against me, as you once did,
my head in the nook there
between shoulder blade and ribcage.

Why this surfacing of your body now,
when in the last years our worn selves
could hardly approach each other?
Why burning when burning
has reduced you to dust?

It's bitter today. Those allowed to shiver,
shiver, and the salt sea licks against its shore.
The chapping is general.

Think of Keats, soon to be cut down,
writing the end as a tender fall sun
filling grapes with sweetness, fields shorn
to make way for the next rising grain.

I can't add you to the compost
and worms which yield
such fragile spring lushness.

Not while I still place you here,
on a November night under the lamp,
taking me onto your lap, your big girl—
while my arms wrap your head.
We laugh, but we hold tight.

Salvage

*Your death my own held breath at the bottom
of the pool.*
                    Robert Fanning

I gleam. I mourn.
                    Tess Gallagher

The Cruelest Month

Clouds seal the sky
in April twilight,
dusk's entrance

a gradient of subtraction.
Sun has its chance
when it sinks low enough

to slant beneath the overcast,
compressed to thick color
like the everywhere-burst

of Big Leaf Maple buds.
For moments, my favorite
season seems to quiet me.

Here, among my plantings,
your death is nothing more
than how light changes—

fierce flare, half shadow.
I make the difference,
full of missing,
          face lit by gold.

Comfort

Swift as a shadow, short as any dream…
so quick bright things come to confusion.
       A Midsummer Night's Dream, 1.1. 149

1
How often you just left me
to figure things out. I was fierce enough.

Before I can scatter them,
wind seizes your few ashes.
You might have chosen this peak,
Grand Valley below,
lakes jeweled along it like lapis lazuli.

I want a Tibetan Sky Burial, you
always teased, your body
to nourish the birds.

Last day of summer, I resist—what I'm best at—
tomorrow's coming rain.
Two seasons since your death.

How you *could* comfort me.
Today as the tears stuttered out and I quieted,
it would be a small ironic remark
about the world's cruelty, maybe your arm
reaching around. Out of the pack

would come special chocolate.
Or a nice chunk of cheese. You'd have to take
your arm away to neatly slice and spear
and ferry a piece to my mouth.

2
Remember the summer we finally made it
to Hayden Pass—where you'd been headed
since the time your stepfather began the trek

without a tent? When the night deluge came,
your down bag a sponge,
you chucked it into his illegal fire
and trekked home.

That disappointment drove you up the last
steep grade, rushing on without me,
my *stop* foundered on this same wind.

Your looking back didn't mean
we had to lose each other.
You could walk down,
help me to the summit,

your saved Eurydice. You pillowed
our jackets in the hollow of broken basalt,
so I could lie down,

eat summer sausage from your pocketknife.
We showed each other the view.

3
The afternoon you died, drenched white-green
of a perfect April poured over what you had been.
Primal light you loved.

Today sinks in deep-heated haze,
as if the sun had all the time in the world
to loiter among its yellowed grasses and polish them.

Behind me, solid ridges row toward Olympus,
the nearest bristling its sawblade of firs.
It's hard to feel our earth floating on liquid fire.

Salvage

compensation paid for lives and property
something valuable extracted, as from rubbish

You loved disassembly,
down to wheels, screws, bolts, washers,
remains of old industrial kitchens
sorted into reused coffee cans and garage-sale buckets,
stacks of wood wrenched from a condemned house,
or a board sawn true out of twisted grain—
a tree's disease.

Each thing stripped to its essence,
potential of becoming,
you saw yourself as a man
defying consumption and needless waste.
Rescue. Setting things free,
their scars a burnishing.

You'd only been dead four months.
3,400 pounds of metal lay in the side driveway.
Not counting two cars.
Fred, who hauled it away to his scrap yard, Fred who
        didn't
know me but could stand in the sunlight
and say, *I understand how it is.*
He had lost his five-month
granddaughter to SIDS.

What you were going to do always ran
far ahead of what happened
since you couldn't seem to salvage self, often told me
I'd taken on damaged goods.

I tried to hold back accumulation,
make space for you to reassemble yourself
into the humming present,
a tenable music.

That harmony would mean deserting
the heavy, cumbersome saw parts of the thirties,
    stand-ins
for those people from your past,
ruined, abused, alcoholic, scorned,
cheated out of their property,
your mother forcing your child self
to be a man
after your dad left.

That each thing, each person,
would win a ransomed place in the world,
released from blame. You too.
My words run on, pretending
they can stand for what isn't here,
lives we saved from the wreck,
and polished,
honed the pain to yield.

Fear of their Eating our House Alive

uncovering your wood

Some Saturdays—this was the 80s—
you couldn't resist
cutting more choice boards

in the log yards, awash in old growth,
where weekdays you ran the office.
Our basement was full.

You must have known
storing rough-cut in the woods,
even stickered, was a gamble.

I cut this wood, all you said to me,
the shrouded reserves,
some map to your future.

When you died, the stack
under its tangled vines and rotten tarp
still seemed whole.

But twenty years of your fierce
guarding was plenty
for armies of carpenter ants

to hollow the layers and nest.
As I carried off the top boards,
life appeared, thousands in roiling

masses. Deeper and deeper.
They grabbed their eggs
from the nurseries and ran.

I had to spray them down.
Clearing away what can't be saved—
my job. I'll turn the salvage

to firewood, spread the rest,
as they do, hastening spoiled wood
into earth for more trees.

Past the mulch
roots drill deep, ants too,
reclaiming their remnants.

Danger of the Flying Wheels

I want the *iron* of you, the strength in those small,
    slender hands
which could open anything.
Joking with my friends in our hallway,
did you know? Lurking that afternoon minute by
    minute *closer*—
death's *machinery*,
which later seems irresistible, inevitable.

What I found in the dark, your body,
would have seemed inexplicable if it had been living, if
it had only been hiding, the way it is hidden now,
gathered from me into the *iron* coldness
of shock each time I think of you.

You come to me any moment I *stand* still.
Tarry, old as Chaucer. I want you to *tarry*
and come *close, father* of our child, she who needs
    more *father*.

That great *machinery*,
special work of the cell, which makes one from two
instead of two from one—in our daughter,
indivisible, inescapable. She carries us, as the being
we always strove to become but couldn't. *Gathered*
    ourselves,
stretched, but were always two selves—

You and I had to make *iron*, gears,
come *closer* and in the danger of the flying wheels,
    the meshing teeth,
push into the sparks *together*, unafraid.

Inquiry

the crowner hath sate on her
Hamlet 5.1.4

The coroner dallied: an inspector had to be hauled over
from the next peninsula. Then came the weekend,
when no one worked, you zipped into a body bag,

sealed by the sheriff. Nearly a week
before the inquiry was over. When you'd been cleared,
I'd been cleared, I remembered

that night you were wearing the old herringbone
shirt-jacket Lisel loved because it was retro.
Clutching your empty urn, I focused on asking

for the shirt. The mortician raised his eyes
to test how I might be, then hazarded,
I couldn't remove it now. It would tear skin.

Welded into your clothes, you needed me
to hurry the unlocking fire. I held out the urn.
Ok, I said, tearing skin. *Forget the jacket.*

Sweeping

a few years after my husband died, our house burned

Sweep up the little scraps now
and set them away.

Your grown daughter is crying.

We rarely speak of the house fire.
Her child is among us.
Oh, that burned, we say
as if nothing mattered but this child.

We chat about our dead
husband, father, and grandfather
as if he sits among us
drinking his tea.

Your daughter is weeping.
Important things were lost,
not just beds, couches, crammed bookcases.

Sweep those up.

Tears like rain soak the ashes
to unwieldy lumps. Immovable.
Sweep and let these be each day's burden.

Was there a time when waking
was to the present?
Grant the children those days.

When the floor is swept, tomorrow
we sweep again.
Loss doesn't ennoble.

Come, we say to the child
cut out the red hearts, paste them
on the cards, one for each classmate,
color the figures.
We'll all work together.

Come. Then we'll ride bikes,
and after that, a snack.

Your grown daughter. It wasn't
the time to put your arms around her.
Maybe, when we are alone.

Both of us know sweeping, the dailiness of brooms.
We give the domestic its due.

The Genesis of Life: 1

They are two figures floating in a dark river, one holding the other on her lap, bending to cradle him and whisper in his ear.
Maaza Mengiste, The Shadow King

Who'd think the moon could pare itself so thin?
Theodore Roethke

The Genesis of Life Lay Deep and Anticipant Under the Sky, 1944

Morris Graves

i

After I held you, dead, in the chilly April dark,
after the sheriff and ambulance,
I went inside and locked the door.

I turned on all the lights.
I climbed the stairs to our bed
and lay on it because hours would have to pass

before gray could come to the windows.
I lay in the dry electric glare.

I went over and over the details,
but nothing emerged.

ii

Graves was jailed for nearly a year, refusing
to serve in World War II.
When they couldn't keep him longer,

he fled to his cabin on Fidalgo Island.
It held the genesis of sky, he wrote.
He painted furiously from his humiliation,
nights too, black waves, sparklered,
as water reaches to the leading moon.

He was painting to get his life back:
the sound carried intensely, he wrote.
*Living alone in the forest, kerosene light,
you spent a lot of time outside, just
listening.*

iii
The genesis of life lies deep, its end
the same. Grief handed out like tides,
indefinable except for change.
Nothing to see, I listen.

You died when light was coming on,
your last reaching-out to help me.

The May dusks which followed
already diffused with exuberant dawns.
I could wake early, so early,
and not be afraid.

Doves and Eagles of the Inner Eye.
In the Moonlight. Graves heard
dark and light, coming and going,
making each other possible,
especially as waves fold through.

Every morning is expectant
and for those unafraid, every night.

Clearcut and the Stumped Sky

Stop time. Stop it growing over the days like blackberry
    vines
twisting their thorns, their spined leaves, through
    scarred ends of logging.
"Heal the eroded land," says the universe.

Stop healing. New shoots snake forward to root down
    anywhere
and begin camouflage. My friends with their empty
    berry buckets
wave to me, time racing along on its dark plump
    rewards.
Afternoons with you, the ones we no longer make
    together,
lose detail, slump into shade.

Stop memory. Somnolent sweetness carries from
    the blackberry maze
inviting my face turned to yours,
our eyes locked in the knowledge we've found
    a mother lode.

Stop memory, which stops with the past.

Stop the way stories have ended: twine and flow from
    breakfast
into lunch, while our house, carried on its sunlit
    afternoon of music,
bends toward dinner talk. Stop the end of old
    camping tales hyped
as rain spatters our tent roof and ruins this trip too.

I have to pick blackberries without you or not at all.

I know you're missing Daddy, says my daughter,
   but some days
you are having a good time, and you should admit that.

A different person is pushing heavy socks into my old
   stained sneakers. I
don't know her, don't dare, as she spreads the days
   like covering vines
into the slash, hiding uneven ground and sudden,
   treacherous holes.

While I keep saying, *Well, what should come next? I mean,
   given all the*
years of me. As the quiet dampness of the great firs,
   stationary
and letting the wind carry their gossip, the great firs,
   earth systems
in themselves, down to the mycorrhizae, are brought
   to ground.

A Patch of Huckleberry

Something about empty ponds
behind the moraines in this drought year
and the distant necklace of lakes
running up Grand Valley.

Adding the times I'd stepped off
from the last of them with you
onto treacherous shale slopes,
then over rills seeping through moss—

Something about how color—
three flaming azaleas and a patch
of red huckleberry—touched steep slopes
pelted in alpine fir,

how sun sparked off one slick precipice.

None of it brought you to sit beside me.
I was the one for a moment
without skin,
like you, ash.

The blaze of your non-being in me
should sear everything, but photos, your tools,
your clothes remain.

Each sharp want, the force of it,
almost, but never reaching you—
the link of our selves walking here.
What belongs to *flesh*.

On the unrelenting climb, again and again
I exhaust myself,

extinguish need,
join the grasses and vanish.

But who would be trusted with a tale
this evanescent?

Fragile

talking to my husband

1
Help me think of the fragility of girls
as they begin to bleed. Away from home,
a high school speech conference,
too ashamed to go boldly to the dispenser
and put my quarter in, I wound toilet paper
over and over the one pad
I had for emergency.

These girls, torn from families, guilty I suppose,
serve detention. For each three tampons
handed out, they must present their three used ones.
Their most private splayed out for the world—
what I feared at fifteen.

Fragile, your words
on the birthday card you gave me
almost a year before you died,
two elegant cranes gilded, paired.
I have many regrets in my life.
You are not one of them,
you wrote, realizing
you were at the end of a road,
only a few things had worked for you.

Letting me know in your way,
these words were the same
you once scrawled boyishly, extravagantly,
on the back of a note early on:
Who wants to be the important man
in your life? I do.

I've lost you and our house.
I comb through the fire's remains,
the cranes not among them.

A friend says, *Rescue that lost moment,*
bring it back, imagine it as only you can.

Late winter, wild plums are blooming,
candle licks among the bare maples and cherries.
Little birds come to the feeder,
nothing flashy, juncos, sparrows.

2
In my teenage years I didn't
find the gaggle of girls
who would have got me laughing
over the blood we'd have to shed,
worked the dispenser for me.

Warmth was the best part
of our life as a couple
and a certain understanding,
that we both,

loving extravagantly our own daughter,
would care how these girls banded
together, asking the public for redress.

During the news, we'd cheer them on.
Rescued, their lives might find a flourishing,
as we did, even one person
to go arm-in-arm.

The Genesis of Life: II

We must be patient,
but I cannot choose but weep to think they would
lay him in the cold ground.
    Hamlet 4.5.68-70

until we are like the dead pouring water for the dead
unaware that our slender thirst
is unquenchable.
    Tess Gallagher

Those Were the Times,

driving home from weekly shopping
the farm way.
Our treat of chocolate biscotti beside us,
we loitered by the fallow fields,
along the seed orchard, talked about new books
or politics, car heater warming us,
the kind of talk that thirty years before
had brought us together.

As the first hot sip of grocery-store coffee
turned into lukewarm,
and our cookie disappeared, I always
thought: how short the pleasures are.
Soon we'll be home unpacking,
turning away to weekend chores.

The day you died just like that.
"I'll get these," as you always said,
bringing in the heavy bags
while I filled the fridge, each time
delighted a man would help me.
Five brothers and a dad—in two decades,
no one moved in my direction.

You "kicked up" the stovefire, got ready
for your afternoon of sawing wood.
As we separated, I had no inkling.
Did you? None of us think we'll be called
to death.

Are the pleasures shorter than all the rest?
Hot coffee cooling turns bitter,
but behind its heat was always bitterness.
An acquired taste.

Nothing gold can stay, says Frost,
as if the losing is what counts—
We took our chances.
Daring the end.

Canyon

Never the same,
fog drapes itself over ridges,
brushes a Chinese scroll.

Today's smudged fall sun
brightens without heat.
Like your death,

a shower of dying sparks.
Red tail, eagle, vulture
careen through the corridor,

high above the creek,
level with our house on the rim.
Leaves gone, maple keep

their grip on the precipice. Wind
rouses their branches to a naked
clattering.

Canyon is the deep crevasse
which gathers. Everything
as sexual: rain falls here

on the edge and far into the deep,
calling steelhead.
They run source-ward,

as our reveling did, moments
we joined them against that
current rushing to the sea.

Reading "Grief" by Louise Erdrich

After I found you dead on the ground,
after the sheriff took your body away,
I went into the house and turned on
the lights. They shone out,
but I couldn't see
the warm windows inviting.

I lay on our bed in all my clothes.
As I've lain nights since,
sometimes covered, sometimes not.
Lain without you, that shine
of your body heat reaching out
as light streams through windows.

Leaving home in the dark,
I've passed house after house—
the lighted windows like longing.
Our family, at dinner,
talking over wine, reading,
but in the same room.

Two nights in a row,
a full, close moon,
wolf moon, haunted the fog.
It woke me, and I got up, unafraid
to walk toward it, spilling
through the window.

No wolves. No coyotes. No sound.
Moon's light icy as January.
Waking me. Keeping me awake,
like the bright squares from houses.
Their offers.
Insistent against dark.

Working the Light to
Imagine the Making,

though it's January. Gray presses us down.

Was it just a trick of light that caught
your black hair to your shapely head,
gleamed me to you,
made me wife, then mother?

Even smudged, our star touches clouds
with definition, shapes lying against each other
like spent lovers, the lounge of being.

Work the light now, I tell my dreams:
that in the luster/shadow of foliage or cedar fans
you would emerge again,
sun catching your glasses.

But when I reach to hug you
as you walk upshore of me on a bouldered beach,
my hands press through cloud flesh.
I've got to go, you say, and point to the man,
your father, already walking on,
washed in muted beach light.

It's a landscape of rainbows, someone said
of our rain-fed peninsula. Water working cloud-light
lets us imagine gold just out of reach,

as memory ignites in the drift of brightness
opening onto this ledge above the canyon
where our house sits as if a family still
woke to work and school,
then gathered for the coveted talk over dinner.

That kindling says you *couldn't* be gone.

Your hair turned totally white
by the time I lost you,
and making was in my hands.

Sun's covered again, as mostly it's just
the drops themselves—not light
stitched onto them,

leaden light, fog-dome light still working.

The Genesis of Life: III

*Es gibt nichts, was uns die Abwesenheit eines uns lieben
Menschen ersetzen kann und man soll das auch garnicht
versuchen; man muss es einfach aushalten und durchhalten;
…denn indem die Lücke wirklich unausgefüllt bleibt, bleibt man
durch sie miteinander verbunden,…Man trägt das vergangene
Schöne nicht wie einen Stachel, sondern wie ein kostbares
Geschenk in sich.*
                    Dietrich Bonhoeffer

*There is nothing which can replace the absence of a person
we love, and we shouldn't even try. We have to humbly endure
and persevere;…because when the absence remains unfilled,
then through it we are still joined to our loved one…We carry
the absent loved one in ourselves not as a thorn but as a
precious gift.*
                    trans. Alice Derry

Clearwater, Once More

It's all up or down. Struggle up one hill,
down another, cross the canyon thicketed
with willow and yellow currant, steering clear
of poison sumac, up, then down, switchbacks
where the downside foot, braking, always cramps.

Time collapses. As if it were twenty years ago,
mom and dad alive, I'm walking the desert hills
which surround their house. From their summits,
these hills finger into canyons carved by rivulets
running to the river now. Dry in summer.

White bleeding heart, four kinds of lomatium,
balsam root. Close-up, the hills glow yellow.
My brothers and I have come for shooting stars,
magenta bits hidden in last year's bunch grass—
nothing there unless you know it.

When she was four, walking beside me,
my daughter planned our tea party
under this earth after I died. She would
"come to me," and we'd be together, as always.
She's grown now, and married, a mother.

Wind. The bite of March cold.
My husband dead. I stumble on uneven rocks
hidden in the new green, give myself to earth as I fall
so I will go lightly, curve into the hillside,
not break. Earth-covered, I clamber up again.

Free of star thistle and still-denned rattlers,
spring is the time of hills, summer the river,
flowing below us, this valley's heart.

Thirty years on, dams have stolen its steelhead
and the white-sand beaches.

Tamed, it meets the tamed Snake. But from this
　　hilltop,
its dark, comforting stripe, and across to Lapwai,
clear up the snowy Waha, looks the same.
My daughter and I still talk lightly
about sitting at a festive table,

her father with us, Clearwater above. I can't think
of a better explanation. I follow my brothers:
coats off when the sun warms us
under a sheltering cliff. Coats on
when we curve back single-file into the wind.

Companion

together with bread

*our government has been unable to locate
the parents of 534 children separated
at the southern border crossing*

Like the meadow grasses,
sere, I come to this trail,
a favorite of yours, high narrow ridge
deep in, to find you—

after I've felt drawn to them on a day
when smoke from southern wildfires
has ghosted the mountains,

a hot day which should be crisp autumn.
Pandemic. Race riots.
Hikers masked.

Breathing the burned air,
my body remembers:
thirty-four years ago we stood here,

our daughter ready
to make her entrance,
my belly tight, hard as stone.

Surely on a day when our joining
would soon be evident,
indivisible in one being,

surely I could find you here,
not just the worn-out memories
I marshal in their familiar line-up,

but you, yourself. I miss you
more than ever when I cross
the huckleberry meadows
seared scarlet.

At home, still sorting your things,
I found a plaque the *pro bono* lawyers
gave you, "for your efforts
to improve access to justice
for those in need." Walking with them,
with me, side by side.

Our country at a crossroads
again: killing those with dark skin—
our long practice of lynching—

separating brown children
from their parents.

Say their names.
But we don't know them,
haven't been given a way to find them.

Lunch was always part of our walking,
sitting where we could see
all the wild ridges, their steep
rises and falls, the way they piled
up toward Olympus. Lunch
with a keen appetite, sharpened by
that one coming toward us,
our search for her name.

You spread out the jackets
so I could sit in comfort, you sliced
the apples and cheese, broke
the chocolate for us. Together.

More Light,

you always vowed
were Goethe's last words.

Hummingbird whirring at the feeder,
vulture, high coasting,

both seize this sparse
February twilight.

I know you couldn't help
leaving me.

On this night, decades ago,
we first slept together, two

hungry bodies, then the trusted
back-to-back in sleep.

I've no real way
to get out of this life.

No courage there.
Lying if I said I didn't

want to be with our daughter.
Our grandson. You remember,

for a little while to be the one
adored, doing everything right.

When he says, *Ama,*
come live with me forever, I want to.

Forget sleep for a while,
my love, come to me.

Thoughts, dreams,
anyway you can.

Notes to the poems

Hamlet

I taught *Hamlet*, my favorite Shakespeare play, many times over forty years of teaching. Memorization is not my strong suit, but after teaching the play and watching various film and live renditions, lines from *Hamlet* popped up everywhere in my daily life because they were so appropriate. They became part of our family dialogue.

Always the enigma, what is the play about? Always the question, even from people who don't believe in murder, why did he take so long to act? Yet any rational person might "hesitate" before murdering someone, especially on a ghost's advice. And as Claudius learns throughout the play, something we are still learning in modern times, regime change doesn't work. Isn't *Hamlet* supposed to be Shakespeare's answer to the popular revenge plays of the day? Critics I read kept getting tangled in Freudian impulses, or denigrated Hamlet, Ophelia, and the play's wide-ranging structure.

When my husband died, the fog of questioning resolved itself. The play depicts grief. Hamlet no longer seems weak and vacillating, or misogynistic, Ophelia, victim-like. Every action of both these lovers is a sign of grieving, especially young grief with no support from adults around them. Sudden, inexplicable anger, especially about unrelated things, depression, feelings of going crazy, suicide wishes, uncontrolled impulses, mood changes accompanied by torrents of words—I felt them all, even surrounded by friends and family.

Living with the shock of my husband's sudden death, I thought each poem in this manuscript might find its way to the play, but that didn't happen. Other plays also crept in. Nevertheless, I want to honor Hamlet by pointing out the references which did occur:

At the Edge of a Dream: 2.2.210

Harvest: 4.3.20

Ghosts: Hamlet: 1.3.32; 1.2.85; 3.4.124; *Romeo and Juliet*: 3.2.82; *A Midsummer Night's Dream*: 5.1.16-17.

I Wake, then Drift: 5.1.263

references are to *The Wadsworth Shakespeare*, second edition.

Other notes:

"I Stand in Color": Linda Gregg writes, "A faith in the flowers, a faith / in the chosen masters of saving / what to keep and what to throw away."

"Danger of the Flying Wheels": The poem began with words from a favorite Sharon Olds poem.

"Your Death Invades Me": During the earliest days of grief, I read novel after novel, in this case, *Lila* by Marilynne Robinson and *The Master Butchers Singing Club* by Louise Erdrich.

"*The Genesis of Life Lay Deep and Anticipant Under the Sky, 1944*": Graves took his title from Beryl Markham's *West with the Night*.

"Working the Light": I used a line by Elizabeth Woody to start the poem.

About the Author

Asking is Alice Derry's sixth full collection of poetry.
Her fifth book *Hunger* appeared from MoonPath
Press in 2017. Her fourth book *Tremolo* appeared
from Red Hen in 2012. Tess Gallagher writes of
the book: "*Tremolo* is a tour de force of vibratory
power that marks Alice Derry as having come into
her own as one of our very best poets." *Strangers
to Their Courage* (Louisiana State University Press,
2001), was a finalist for the 2002 Washington Book
Award. Li-Young Lee writes of *Strangers*: "This book
… asks us to surrender our simplistic ideas about
race and prejudice, memory and forgetfulness, and
begin to uncover a new paradigm for 'human.'"
Stages of Twilight (Breitenbush, 1986), won the King
County Publication Award, chosen by Raymond
Carver. *Clearwater* appeared from Blue Begonia
Press in 1997. Derry has three chapbooks: *Getting
Used to the Body* (Sagittarius Press, 1989), *Not As You
Once Imagined* (Trask House, 1993), and translations
from the German poet Rainer Rilke (Pleasure Boat
Studio, 2002).

Derry's M.F.A. is from Goddard College (now
Warren Wilson). She is Professor *Emerita* at
Peninsula College, Port Angeles, where she directed
the Foothills Writers Series for three decades. In

2013, she helped plan the 75th Raymond Carver Birthday Celebration and delivered its keynote address; in 2017, she was Peninsula College's 17th Writer in Residence. With colleague Kate Reavey, she has also facilitated writing workshops for area tribes. She lives and works on Washington's Olympic Peninsula. Her website is: www.alicederry.com.

CPSIA information can be obtained
at www.ICGtesting.com
Printed in the USA
JSHW042122250822
29669JS00004B/22